EAGLE & PHENIX

ALSO BY NICK NORWOOD

Gravel and Hawk
A Palace for the Heart
The Soft Blare
Text (limited edition, with Erika Adams)
Wrestle (limited edition, with Erika Adams)

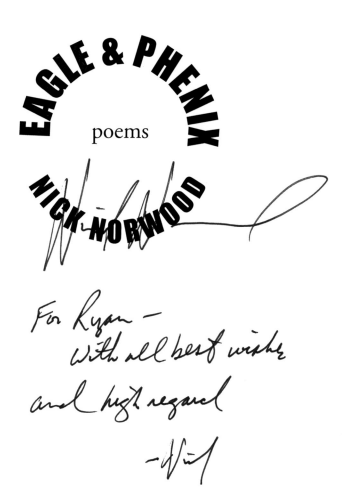

EAGLE & PHENIX

poems

NICK NORWOOD

*For Ryan —
With all best wishes
and high regard*

— Nick

Snake Nation Press
Valdosta, Georgia 2019

Snake Nation Press, the only independent literary press in south Georgia, publishes *Snake Nation Review*, a book of poetry by a single author each year, and a book of fiction by a single author each year. Unsolicited submissions of fiction, essays, art, and poetry are welcome throughout the year but will not be returned unless a stamped, self-addressed envelope is included. We encourage simultaneous submissions.

Published by Snake Nation Press
110 West Force Street
Valdosta, Georgia 31601
Printed and bound in the United States of America.
Copyright © Nick Norwood 2019
Cover art by Margee Bright Ragland
Cover and text design by Justin Briley
Author photos by Tamma Smith
All Rights Reserved

ISBN: 978-0-9979353-4-9

for Susan

; it is spring by Stinking River where a magnolia tree, without leaves, before what was once a farmhouse, now a ramshackle home for millworkers, raises its straggling branches of ivorywhite flowers.

~William Carlos Williams

Contents

I

Povre je suis de ma jeunesse.

~François Villon

RONNIE'S

Dad dead, Mom—back in the bank, tellering—
started dressing in cute skirts and pants suits
she sewed herself from onionskin patterns
and bright-colored knits picked up at Cloth World.
Got her dark brunette hair cut in a shag.
And she and her single girlfriends from work
on a weekday night would leave me to "Love
American Style" or Mary Tyler Moore
and step out to hear the country house band
or now-and-then headliners like Ray Price
and Merle Haggard. Mom's blue Buick Wildcat
shoulder-to-shoulder with the other Detroit
behemoths in the dim lot around back.
Wind skittering trash along the street. Bass
notes thumping through the sheet-metal walls
and the full swinging sound suddenly blaring
when a couple came in or out the door.
I know because I'm there, now, in the lot,
crouched behind the fender of a Skylark
or Riviera, in the weird green glow
of the rooftop *Ronnie's* sign, not keeping tabs
on Mom, not watching out, just keeping time
with the band and sipping a Slurpee
while she dances through this two-year window
before getting re-hitched, settling back down.
Just twenty-seven, twenty-eight years old,
looking pretty, and having the time of her life.

LATCHKEY

Remember the first time
you let yourself in—
stunned by the sheer
silence of it all,

the sunlight blooming
on mute, blank-faced
walls. And how you
stormed, then,

from room to room
blistering furniture
and framed photographs
with your hollering,

commanding the sunlight
to go away go away
because you wanted
to be alone.

Remember how you
yelled yourself
dizzy—exhilarated
and scared.

And how eventually
you dropped
into your mother's chair
and watched

that same sunlight creep
silently across floors,
up walls,
and let itself out.

OLD SCHOOL

The second hand sweeps its sonar
above the blackboard's ocean.

Bolt the instant the bell blasts
and blur past Big Nina, Bob Harris.

Round the horn of the first row,
out the door and into the hall,

empty but for one lone lane—
a waxed gleam—two, maybe three

more seconds before other doors
open, disgorge. Controlled sprint

to the opposite end, into the stairwell,
down a flight, hip-check the exit bar

and bang wide the metal door,
burst into the cold gray air,

into the light, under the sky. Be
first off the schoolyard, because

you have to be. Because otherwise
there'd be Johnny McNair dry-

humping you while others howl.
Fists, kicks, snot in your mouth.

A bloody shirt you'd have to explain.
Your sister's birdlike smirks.

First, then, out the gate, down
streets of barking dogs, laundry

on a line, the postman noticing you
for the hundredth time. Around

the corner, home, into your room.
And—soft, slow—close the door.

ORIENTATION

His family owned a cabin by the lake.
We rented the little white frame next door
to the house in town, earned an invitation:
June, sun, swimming, a Chris-Craft runabout.

But what's lingered most is the trip we took,
the two of us, afoot, to the bait shop
and back, along a trail between a pasture
and a stretch of woods. He made me lead,

though he was the host, older, knew the way.
Then ducked out, behind some trees, I guess,
when I wasn't looking, left me alone
among a small herd of black angus cows.

Not long after, his family sold, moved
to a house in a tony subdivision
farther from riffraff like us. There'd be no
more lazing on the warm planks of a pier.

I looked both ways, called out his name.
Nothing. Mute trees. Cows chewing cuds.
And what I see now's the blaring sunlight,
defining the hardwood trunks, mesquite.

It glosses the cowhides and silvers grass
under its glare. The path back home's
no longer a mystery, exposed, a band
of red clay as clear as a trail of blood.

Tar Road

Come June this brook runs soft,
takes its lumps, before the family
gets AC, your cheap bike busted,
walking tar-heeled, skin-to-skin
with a bruise-black two-laner hot
and spongy underfoot. Everything
existing, it seems like, on a one-
to-one basis. You here, the sun there,
the dark road. An oak, another oak.
The deaf mute's pitiful house.
A shack, a shed, your uncle's trailer.
Up ahead, the creek, its drowned
tires like rings of tar flash-cooled
in the au lait water, crawdads
to catch on cotton string, ease out
of the brown ooze, haul home
in a bucket, let stink on a step.
Your feet reading road like Braille,
the woman with a radio always
eyeing you from her slack porch,
porch-swinging in 4/4 time. Under-
ground, a dark crude sea atilt
against the earth's axis, while
at your back, the *twang-twang*
of AM country steel guitar,
then a crow cawing country blues.
A *twang-twang*. A *twang-twaaaang*.
A road disappearing into woods.

SHETLAND

Shorty, lone grazer of Granddaddy's pasture,
brawny, bristle-maned chestnut stuffed with clover,

our horse: intractable, brutish, and mean.
But once, when I was about eight or nine,

I found him idle by the barbwire fence,
just staring—calm, inert—toward the house,

and got a wild hair, thought, *I'll stroke his muzzle.*
Sidling up, whispering, I put palm to skull—

an anvil, a fieldpiece shrink-wrapped in hide—
and his story traveled up my arm. This cloud

of sweat and flies and moist, long-rifled breathing,
this piss-hot leathery stink, had *being.*

I was resolved to spend all day with Shorty,
worried it'd be the only time he'd let me.

He was a rough beast, I a skittish child.
But for once, now, we two were reconciled

and my brain forged for us an island north,
hardships braved, friendships kept, galloping forth.

A rousing age that passed in half an hour.
I heard through the screen door a radio stir,

crackle, and settle on the local news,
wandered away in dew-soaked tennis shoes.

ANCIENT ART

Deep in the master bedroom,
at the back of the babysitter's house,
between headboard and wall,
was a crawlspace I discovered
just big enough for a child.

I crouched with crayons to write
on the Masonite backing,
my name scrawled repeatedly
like the overlapping images
of deer and bison at Lascaux.

And as with that cave into which
a dog fell seventeen millennia
deep to illuminate the world,
furniture movers of a new millennium
alerted the middle-aged daughter

to the works of a graffitist—
before they were hidden again
to protect them from human breath,
vandals and philistines. But
her mention of them to me

returned whole worlds of secrecy,
silence and semi-darkness,
the nubby feel of crosshatching
transmitted through a stylus,
smell of wood and burnt umber.

Haunted House

"Nature is a haunted house. . . ."
~Emily Dickinson

They carted us there in station wagons.
A tweak this way or that
and we might have missed the place
you could put your ear to

and hear the universe whisper:
a slack Victorian overrun
at Halloween by shrieking children,
shaking and wobbling on its pier

and beam. A tunnel snaked across
its lower floor just big enough
for a kid to crawl through, lined
with shag carpet, 90-degree turns

without warning. Deep inside
you were struck with a panic beyond
what its jake leg builders could've had
in mind, like discovering gravity.

Some giggled, others screamed, as when,
years later, during a total eclipse
the moon's planetary shadow swung to
and blotted out the sun.

II

... and here, their home; and they have gone;
and it is now my chance to perceive this. ...
~James Agee

SMALL FAMILIES: AN ODE

When two sets of grandparents
have only four kids between them,
and those four kids only five,

and the eldest of them, for reasons
never quite clear, disappears,
chooses to live his life in exile,

and his younger brother, though
everyone knows where he lives,
chooses to stay to himself,

the other cousin, an only child,
is impossible to get along with,
and there are the standard doses

of divorce, illness, death, it doesn't
keep Christmas from coming:
the faux fir with its string of lights

and tumble of presents underneath,
a forced, stumbling gratitude,
last year's reused ribbons and bows,

and the kind of too-sugary treats
always in danger of crumbling,
falling apart, in your fingers.

GREAT-GRANDMOTHER

A lioness so stalks your gaze
in the framed photograph we've kept,
taken before 1925, the year
you died at 34, hair swept up

and back, forehead China,
cheekbones high, sharp cliffs,
it seems impossible you're dead,
bones denuded long before

even my mother was born.
And so I stare at you, standing
beside the mild seated husband
who'd outlive you fifty years,

hand on his shoulder, leaning
forward, running a long, straight
shaft through my mortal guts.
Then ages past me.

i.m. Josephine "Josie" Westbrook Tidwell

Great-Grandfather

His second wife cut his hair
sitting in a kitchen chair
under an elm tree in the yard,
their house in an ess-curve

out a county road. Her
quilting frame, hovering hip-
high in the front room, boxed
a gaping hole in sour air.

The nineteenth century hung there.
When he spoke I turned
and ran, spooked by the smell,
his papery skin. Last time

I saw him, he passed me
on the street—a surprise—
looking lost and not knowing
who I was even when

I called his name. Courteous,
distant, he asked the way
to some place I had never
heard of, then wandered on.

i.m. James Benjamin Tidwell

CLEAN SWEEP

After the dance, in the murky light
of a single closet bulb in 1956,
she takes off her dress, hangs it but
neatly, goes to rinse out her socks

and wash her face. Then,
with a damp rag, she wipes down
her shoes, both outside and in,
and pairs them perfect as twins

before climbing into bed. Years later,
after nursing school and marriage
to the engineer, widowhood
and decades of keeping the house

they built in '69 so neat
even the neighbors are impressed,
lying in the lonely king-size
in the final throes of pancreatic,

she directs her niece—the good one,
the one who understands—
to wash the towels, change the spare
room sheets, throw out that stuff

that's in the refrigerator. Curled,
almost fetal, knowing—she must—
it won't be long, she says, Please,
the patio furniture. It's filthy.

i.m. Shirley Mae Norwood Smith

28

AUNT SUE

A tiny base from which you ventured out,
that little town just east of Paris, Texas,
after 45 years of growing up there,
marrying, raising two kids, divorcing. But
big-boned and bossy, hell on cars and cartons
of Kent, you trailed your second husband, "Ron,"
to Colorado. When he left, you stayed,
900 miles from family and friends,
became vice president of the local bank
and lived alone on the outskirts of town,
a tiny base from which you ventured out
to play the slots in rez casinos, bars.
And where your secretary found you in bed,
turned off the television, picked up the phone.

i.m. Eutuana Sue Chesshire Gast

Vietnam Vet

for Maj. Robert Vernon Haney, Ret.

In the silted pools
of his blue-gray eyes

wades a boy in chinos
rolled to his knees

holding a seashell
to his ear, listening

for the ocean. They
told him to listen,

so in good faith
he stands, listening.

ALOFT

It was, for each of them, a maiden flight,
the pair of choppers, as they briefly dipped
over the very fields and pastures where
they'd both grown up, three miles apart, then married
and lived together almost sixty years,
allowing them, in a blurred instant, a glimpse:
the patchwork quilt of it a revelation,
the way the willows furred their winding creek,
the surprising Tonka Toy diorama
and helter-skelter of their neighbors' yards,
ribbon-like narrowness of the county road,
and then, too, as the pilots leveled off,
banking west toward the burn center in Plano,
how quickly it fell away, resolved to sky.

i.m. Canard W. Norwood

Cellphone Image

No sleep in sight, reading, I find, from Einstein,
"The most beautiful thing we can experience

is the mysterious," and I take him at his word.
Still, even that doesn't help me slip back,

and resorting to one of my devices I see
my son Graham in a band of summer sunlight

slanting across my parents' backyard, home
from college, standing with his head slightly cocked,

broad-shouldered and lean, in one of my old
pearl-button cowboy shirts, smiling.

Behind him suburbs fade into gauzy relief,
hardwoods in full summer shag, a wood fence,

one bright white beautiful cloud.
I linger on it, linger and linger, until

the phone itself starts nodding off (like a swath
of dark crepe dropped over the screen). Then

the screen goes black, becomes, that instant,
a mirror. My own tired face stares back.

In a Deer Stand with My Daughter

Because she's nineteen, and because
she wants this, this blood (though
she cannot tell me why), I'm here
to do what I can. We watch a doe
edge across a clearing toward this oak
our seat on stilts is propped against,
fifty yards off and unaware of us,
the .308 across our laps. We stay
still as assassins, Natalee hoping
a big buck is soon to follow. She is
so delicate in her movements
and careful watchfulness, the flickering
of ears and tail, the woods so quiet,
we're startled by the sudden rapping
of a woodpecker. A barred owl's
grunting echoes through the forest.
A crow caws like a circus barker.
Again. Again. Then flies off. I lift
my binoculars, and lo, there he is
at wood's edge, melted into reality,
his modest rack like a small castle
balanced atop his head. Nat eyes
him through her rifle scope. But
it's growing darker, she's in a race
against time, busy willing the buck
to move about half again as close,
commit the last mistake he'll ever make
so we can waft home on his musk,
cut his handsome shape into food,
remember this day till we die. And
darkness is inevitable, the luck
of having such a daughter, some few
late fall afternoons to spend, things
no one can count on. It's in that
reverie I'm lost when she ejects,
with a loud *rat-cha!* the round

from her chamber, sends both
deer bounding—and all of us—
unharmed, into the dusk.

III

When the mills are slack this town is veritably a
place of lost and hungry people.
~Carson McCullers

CLAMOR

The mill's non-stop noise, a whir and a clangor,
follows him home, over the bridge and up
the hill, while at his back it goes on wheezing,
chuffing lint through manifold windows,

into the village with the lunch-bucket knocking
at his knee, to bounce a kid on his knee
in the sunlit parlor of the four-room cottage
identical to the one next door, next door

to the river that powers the turbines. The privy's
sulfurous stench stretches to the porch while
his own open windows pass heat and flies
and rugrats flap through the sprung screen door.

A rung up from the tenant shack, maybe two
from a hovel on the Rhine, a hut on the Liffey,
the Mersey, the Volga, he is equal now
to the terrace-house bloke in Wigan,

to his next-century brother in Coimbatore,
or the one in a cinderblock flat in Nantong
perched above the Yangtze, whose mill tunes
its waters daily to the color it's dyeing—

red, blue, purple—through a little trap door.

THE NAMES

*"Alphabetical List of the Registered Voters
of the City of Columbus, Georgia, 1934"*

Heading on the first page: "White Men."
Proceeding thus: Abbett, Abbott,
Ackerman, Adair, et cetera, for 51

and two-thirds pages. "Occupation":
Conductor, Bookkeeper, Carpenter,
Salesman, Clerk, Mechanic. . . . Then,

for just over two pages, "Colored Men."
Janitor, Porter, Minister, Drayman,
Butler, Driver, Laborer, Custodian,

Teacher. . . . Next, "White Women,"
running some 21 pages, names, ages,
addresses. None with a listed vocation.

Last, "Colored Women": ten names
all told: Ella Brewer, Addie Giddens,
Charlotte Hammons, Tena Hines,

Julia Jarrett, Laura Johnson, Mollie Rogers,
Henrietta Shepherd, Mattie Spencer,
Lettie Williams. A simple ledger,

duly certified by M.M. Affleck,
Clay E. Taylor, and Milton Long,
Registrars, as being "true and correct."

Remains of a Brick Kiln
Built by Slaves

On this stretch of the Natchez Trace
where cars infrequently pass

there's a house that was
an eighteenth-century inn,

a burial ground of unmarked graves.
And there are these relics

a few hundred yards off by themselves
down a faint narrow path through grass:

each among a handful of bricks is buried flush
to the surface like a sinking ship

in that last buoyancy of air trapped
near cabin and stateroom ceiling

before the prow dips and the hull slides
toward the deep bottom. The ground

is ready to take them in,
hide them mostly undisturbed,

haunted only by creatures that mine
the darkness. Crows and jays bark

from black limbs. The sun
in its hovering

seems conspicuous by its silence,
peering through pine boughs

as though quietly observing
those who have stopped to observe.

Velázquez Auto Repair

Pewter at night. A wall clock
above the bench: twenty-four
seven. Brake dust, grease, oil.
At center: the tire machine,
its altar, hymned over hourly
by arm and hammer. Just now,
only the clock hums, goes on
advertising and being ignored
even after hours, the liquid
light oozing from its white
plastic face the only stop
to total dark. The concrete floor
onto which the bloodbath
of fluids daily pours. The rich,
delicious, solvent stench.
Hanging: a rag on a fender
beside a dull glint, ropes of chain
from the engine hoist, an eight-
year-late lurid calendar.
The stillness. And there,
the master, Velázquez himself,
alert and pensive as a painter,
staring out from left of center.

LB on the Violin

Or fiddle, in appliance-service blues,
        Larry in red script over his right breast,
    half a shirttail out, grease stains at the knees,
only the nerdy black glasses aslide

on his nose hinting at the kid he was
        growing up on a pig farm in Ashdown,
    Arkansas, this ball-capped deer-hunting father
of four, repairman of Frigidaires, Whirlpools,

Maytags, and Amanas, wrench-turner née
        class clown, amid the Tuesday grind and clamor
    of the repair shop hid behind swinging doors
back of the appliance store's gleaming showroom,

leaning against an oily workbench lit
        by banked fluorescents suspended on chains,
    his fellow gearheads whooping at this latest
of LB's legendary capers, calling out requests:

"Bob Wills!" "Nah, man—'Devil Went Down to Georgia.'"
        Until LB tunes up and begins to chord,
    the battered relic tucked under his chin,
a sudden serious set to his lips,

his eyes fixed on something invisible
        hovering at waist level above the floor:
    a few strains of some simple cowboy song
that speed up into a bluegrass breakdown

and lilt into a Beethoven sonata
        played imperfectly but with the clear ring
    of having once been practiced, learned, sure-felt;
rich keening notes that seem so alien

here, the room itself, thrust into relief,
          blooms into a state of the hyperreal:
     a clutter of tools and machinery,
triaged washers and dryers with mouths agape,

the syrupy tang of transmission oil
          and unsentimental quality of light.
     It makes the other servicemen stop working
altogether and listen, bemused, become

an audience of music lovers with odd
          heart-happy smiles on their smudged, sweating
     faces, eyes fixed on Larry, then carried up
into the steel-beam rafters of the room

where their focus hangs momentarily
          before returning to their workbenches—
     returning, even as the notes keep climbing,
to the grime of their wrenches, their parts.

HIRED HAND

Jimmy Woodall, Jimmy Woodall,
who drove Granddaddy's tractor
and lived alone in a rented house
busting out its window screens,
why'd you furnish the parlor
with castoff ladies shoes lined up
in furrows, dainty dress-ups
with buckles and straps, an empty
can of Pearl on a windowsill,
walls robin's egg blue? Outside,
where fields' ribs showed through,
a snaking red dirt drive like the veins
in your arms first forked, then
ended at your rusted-out truck.

Jimmy Woodall, Jimmy Woodall,
who rubbed your hand's bony washcloth
over an aching head, lit a smoke,
and mounted the Massey Ferguson,
who knew but me and you
you left a crop of pumps and wedges
to wait on the hardwood floor
while you rumbled from turnrow
to turnrow, the tractor's diesel
throbbing through the iron seat,
your hands on the wheel at ten
and two, backbone rigid, Salem
adangle, until, at last, sunset
swathed the sky in pastel hues?

HAUL

Their two-ton Jimmy staggers now,
rolls and wobbles on creaky springs,
creeping over berms on a rutted
two-track with a house of hay

on its back, is inched back
through a doorway just big enough
to let it in, driver climbing out
and crawling under the flatbed

to enter the hell that is this barn,
a hundred-and-twenty-degree
corrugated-tin oven, air
a vortex of flying debris—

dust, grass, weed, vaporized wood
and dung. To live you must learn
to pivot the weight, to be one
with it: the downswing a free-

fall followed in rhythm by a push
on the upthrust. And thus
it's a thing that can be done,
ninety-pound bales heaved,

chucked into mow, stacked
side-down so as not to burn
(hauler's sacred lore), the last
pair in a row "married" in an al-

most too-tight hole. Daylight
growing incrementally around
the load's unstacked edges.
Then, puffs of fresh air—*thank*

you lord—ice-water slugs,
a dip/smoke/chaw, the swipe
of a bandana across the face.
And then, son, back to square one.

EXTERIORITY

Maybe I'm not very human—
what I wanted to do was to paint
sunlight on the side of a house.
~Edward Hopper

The barn: a Rembrandt inside,
its air mahogany; dust-choked,
hay-flown; reeking of manure,
dried blood, a rich, animal must.

But here, in its dense shade, bales
unloaded and stacked, the old truck
waiting while we smoke, crouched,
with sweat-soaked, crooked backs

propped against the cool tin, we see,
gazing across the yard to the small
wood-frame farmhouse, how sunlight
seethes its white clapboard walls,

stokes it like a bellows, makes it
bloom, and how a mockingbird clings
to the peak of its gable, light,
like light, borne, as it is, on wings.

ABANDONED FARMHOUSE

Its German generations hover
over the floorboards, rise
and swirl in dust clouds kicked up
by footsteps. Nothing else here

but air and echoes, sunlight
slurring through the slumped panes
of sash windows. Each wallowed
stair leads to the second floor,

where the view from bedrooms
stretches toward a brown treeless
horizon sad as a Sunday afternoon.
We creak open the barn, then doors

of a Dodge from the 1940s, grip
its wheel. The radio remains mute,
glovebox gutted as a fish. The seat
covers give up ghosts like an aged

Limburger. Then the house watches
as we walk away, re-abandoned atop
its gentle rise, mouthing goodbyes
in its obsolete vernacular.

IV

Federal forces burned the mill April 17, 1865.
It rose from the ashes in 1866 as Eagle & Phenix
Mills, the added name to signify its rebirth.

~Georgia Historical Commission

EAGLE & PHENIX DAM

I

Ol' Doc Williams dead, down
south the river still stunk
like a sewer, which it was,
the mills' back-alley dye
and mordant dump. Meanwhile,
up the road in Opelika
Martin Ritt set the table
to shoot *Norma Rae*—
the irony of it apparent
only now: cotton-mill
culture had less than
twenty years to live. Gone
all that yelling about unions
over the earsplitting racket
of spinners and looms,
sweating through your bra
and panties, reading thumb-
tacked bulletin boards
on break, lunging lint
all day and slouching home
to a company shack. No
revelations but in things. . . .

II

The midday blast rattled the glass
and made the old mill tremble,
a civic spectacular
viewable via the "Dam Cam"
on the Internet. When the dust

and smoke subsided, the flume
of brickred run its course
in the river current, what was left
was a ragged hole in the heart
of eighteen-eighties' engineering.

The Chattahoochee, freed at *least*
of this one shackle, a hundred
and fifty years of mill culture
drained out of the reservoir;
the flow of blood, sweat, and tears,

released; the gash ripped open.
Then returned a nasty stench,
the sulfurous must of decay
mixed with riverbed mud, dead
fish, cotton-mill chemicals,

and such as the dam kept hid
until the breach brought everything
out in the open. The stink stuck
around about a month, then slowly
dissipated, vanished into air.

But from the powerhouse,
looking down: heart pine timbers
from trees sprouted in the 1600s
and felled in the nineteenth century
lay like a jumble of matchsticks

studded with discarded car parts,
shopping carts, scuttled craft,
dozens of fire extinguishers;
the evolution of Coke, RC,
and Nehi as told through glass

bottles; used tires, toys, tools,
cans, clothing, coins, copper pots,
cell phones; horseshoes, a trumpet,
and a gold ring engraved
GLORIA; iron spikes,

wooden kegs of lead-based paint,
stoneware jugs of shine and cider,
apothecary and cosmetic jars;

a large number of handguns
and knives apparently tossed

from the 13th Street Bridge;
a crucible, acetylene tanks briefly
mistaken for cannon barrels;
and a tangled timeline of lost
fishing gear huddled under

the old headrace like so much
archaeological swag; the lingerings
of which the river, at long last,
would have the pleasure
to wash away. Meanwhile,

III

now that you are here,
amid crag and gleam,

mist-rise and vapor,
dark jade frothing into white lace,

here where the rains come
to gargle, spit jets of spray,

see herons creep, smokestacks
peer through high windows,

spirits sleep—spool and spindle,
shaft and shackle,

Tie-Snake and eagle.
Sit still as the old powerhouse

and mind your moorings,
the river roaring.

THE TIE-SNAKE

Muscogee knew a serpent hid
below the falls in deep water,
glimpsed the Tie-Snake's shadow
beneath the churn and tread.

Spade head solemn as a sphinx.
Untold lengths of scale and strength
coiled and ready to wrap limbs
of fishers and diggers of clams.

Lover who loves only one thing:
to lie with others forever under
froth, amid the crag and gleam
of boulders, the mist-rise and vapor.

Still a handful every year.
A glut of screams, the river's roar
rafters and kayakers paddle over,
ecstatic in their plastic gear.

THREE PALM TREES
ON RAILROAD STREET

Idle under overpasses
Railroad Street runs east
and west a quarter mile
between lonely stretches
of 2nd and 3rd Avenues
separating two possible
if not likely crack houses
from the burned-out husk
of Julius Friedlaender's
wholesale warehouse,
the faded sign painted on
its red brick wall still
advertising jute bagging
and cotton waste
a hundred years late, but
between the railroad
and street after which
it's named, on a strand
of grassless right-of-way,
these three old sailors
of the South Seas—
raggedy, rail-thin, mop-
topped bean poles bend-
ing at the waist as if
stooped by age or rum—
stand in a spaced-out
row a couple hundred
miles from Florida,
paradise untended,
I guess—as I'm about
to pass on my bike—
for upwards of forty
years. They bring me
to a halt. There is no
one around, and what's

around could not be
sadder: a house whose
front door's a blanket,
a trash-strewn gutter,
a Dodge on blocks.
Then these fellows,
their fronds sooty,
graying, and yet bring-
ing me such dingy,
delicious, unexpected
joy, I have stopped
to stare and forget
about where I am
and consider instead
how—however they
came to be—three
of anything make
a row, and how what
survives may bless
by simply being here.

EAGLE-WATCHING

I glassed her again this morning,
pumping upstream on long wing beats,
thrilled at the sudden sight
of her head's hot white blaze.

I gazed across the Chattahoochee
as she skimmed her shadow
over sloped banks crawling with kudzu,
saw her snatch a sunfish

from its given, giving world,
wormhole it out of time mid-swim
and cart it aloft to be stricken
in the bright white air.

On an oak limb her beak-blade went in
eyeball-first while the homeless dozed
on nearby benches, belongings
leaf-bagged beside them.

Elsewhere, I imagined, flags lay limp
against their poles, lights went on
in corporate windows, shoppers waited
to enter big-box stores.

But here, the monarch throned,
cloaked in her dark wings,
while I watched her from a perch
on the opposite bank, binoculars

thrust to my eye sockets, butt
turning stone-cold against
an iron railing. And with a
pivot of her head—methodical,

deliberate—her eyes revolved
toward mine, held them a second,
moved on, while the river rode
silently between us.

BALD EAGLE

after Margee Bright Ragland

I

Head a bright white dome
fitted with a meat-hook,
she sits, helmeted, one
wing crooked to lift, grip

air. She glares, would sooner
steal than hunt. High screamer,
carrion eater, awk-
ward on the ground, she flies

head-down, obeying law;
builds her aerie bigger
piece by piece; spends light years
perched high and still, hawking.

II

Swings, the great kite of her,
down over wide channels,
drags her crooked nails through
the face of the river.

Dusk, sky gone gray, her nest,
a deep cauldron, stews. Cloaked
silhouettes move as humped
shadows, shuffle flaps, still.

Night falls in black silence.
Huddle of stink, her lair,
muddle of meat, bones, scat;
mother's will. And then: the moon.

EAGLE

Jettisoned from the Command Module
on 21 July 1969 at 23:41 UT (7:41 PM EDT)
Impact site unknown
~NASA

Hangs, a tin can with legs,
above the moon's pallor,
floats down like a feather
to plant her feet in chalk.

Out of her, the first man
walks, also the second,
to hop about and speak
brave words about first steps

of men. She squats, remains
womb, sanctuary, home,
until it's time for their
return, to reunite

with *Columbia*. Then
her frail rockets fire just
enough to lift them, leave
that gleaming desolate

soil to which she, lone,
abandoned, will fall back,
crumpling, a heap of foil,
cracked open like an egg.

Phenix City Story

1. November

A local woman, getting on: her bent-
over back pistons like a bellows
as she pumps a broken clawhammer,

beating sense into tenpenny nails
to tack a length of sheeting plastic
over a window frame. She underpins

with scrap tin, cardboard, presswood.
Plucks a fastener from her lips,
pounds it home. Fills cracks

with duct tape, random strips of foam.
Stands back, surveys. She sets
her mouth a certain way and starts

toward the door—then stops
to holler at the little white dog
in its unfenced run, "All right,

Ezekiel. You can come on."
Now, the cozy den: vinyl love-
seat, TV, leaflets from the church.

2. December

The oven's half-open door
slants opposite the gentle slope
of the galled linoleum floor,

all four stovetop burners aflame.
Fumy air trembles over the table,
its fan of utility bills, a cup

of weak coffee and a thick catalog.
The open page: bright plastic
play-pretties the grandbabies

will tear up in two months. The bills
with their prim printed numbers,
the gaudy page. Bills; page. She pulls

the ratty collar of her cardigan
closer, picks up the telephone
and asks a man about the lay-away,

then sets the bills in a neat stack,
puts a rubber band around them,
pencils on the top "Friday week."

3. January

From the bed she hears the ticking
of the five-and-dime clock
in the kitchen. Then the wind

buffeting her plastic sheeting
till the tape tears loose and it starts
to flap. The bedside table

a clot of crumpled Kleenex,
emptied flu-medicine wrappers,
unopened envelopes, she lies

as still as the recently deceased
with newspaper spread over the top
of the coverlet like the people

who have to sleep on the street.
She starts to pray. For her daughter
and grandbabies in California

and for people who sleep on the street.
She says the Amen, Jesus, Amen,
then scours the silence. Clock's stopped.

4. February

She thinks Zeke may have eaten
a hole through the pantry door.
Something's gone bad and reeks.

She's worn a path through the papers
and wadded tissues from bed
to bathroom. She sees her breath

rising in faint humid clouds
through the cold air above her face,
her fever-dizzied head cradled

on a rank pillow. She knows Jesus
had something to do with this.
She knows it was him that sent

the devil as a propane man
to cut her furnace off. It's a sign
He's about to lift her up

out of this bed. It's a sign
she's finally leaving Phenix City.
She sighs, then laughs at herself,

then at something else, she's not
sure what—in her fever. Then,
staring straight up, drifts off.

5. March

The truck from the Salvation
Army has come to haul away
the furniture. She can't

use it. In California?
That sort of thing is beyond
kitsch. She burned the leaflets

and old bills and catalogs
in the rusted trash barrel
out back: they still do that here.

She had to admit, it was kind
of beautiful to watch: the fumes
and bits of feathery paper

wafting up, the dark, thin smoke.
But the stink of it: pure
Alabama. Good riddance,

she thinks, and goodbye. One
last time, goodbye. She settles
her children in the car

with the dog and tries anew
to teach them how to say
its name: *ee-ZEE-ke-ul*.

CHRISTMAS IN COLUMBUS, GEORGIA

A dead ringer for Santa Claus,
he's an aging grease monkey
in a holly-green monkey suit
in the next booth at Burt's
Butcher Shop and Eatery.
Shaggy locks lilting up beneath
a greasy cap, white beard, forking
down his payday sirloin strip
with his plumpety-plump wife.
Friday night, place is packed, a little
awful but cheerful, with its broad-
hipped waitresses, harvest gold
table tops, and working-class folk
digging deep into hearty grub
in wax-papered baskets. The black
couple in the corner's got a kid
six or eight who can't sit still
though Mama says he'd better
till it's time to pay and she
lets him sidle up to St. Nick.
Early December, raw wind
scraping trash across the park-
ing lot, he wants to get his
order in. Santa leans back, smiles,
says he's been watching him, sees
he's being, well, *purty* good.
So all right, what'll it be? Action
figures, a football, lots and lots
and lots of candy. And games.
They part on good terms, the old
man chuckles, downs his sweet tea
while his wife explains to the next
table how it's the same every year.
Another minute more and they're
out the door, climbing in a ten-
year-old Tundra, off to their

white frame in Bibb City, matching
La-Z-Boys, TV. The waitress
refills our cups, my friend springs
for the meal, and I'm off myself
to my workshop in the old mill
to cook up something about
peace, love, and goodwill.

Acknowledgments

Grateful acknowledgment is made to the editors of the following magazines in which some of these poems originally appeared:

Atlanta Review, Blue Collar Review, Concho River Review, Connotation Press, Five Points, The Greensboro Review, The Oxford American, Shenandoah, The South Carolina Review, Southern Poetry Review, storySouth, This Land.

"Latchkey" was reprinted in *Pushcart Prize Anthology XL11* (2018).

"Clamor" was reprinted in *Poetry Daily* (22 February 2014); in *Stone, River, Sky: An Anthology of Georgia Poems* (Negative Capability Press, 2015)—along with "The Tie-Snake," which appeared there for the first time—and in *Science Meets Poetry V* (publication of the Euroscience Open Forum, Manchester, 2016).

"Ronnie's" was reprinted in *American Life in Poetry* (19 September 2016), a syndicated print and online newspaper column written and edited by 2004-2006 U.S. Poet Laureate Ted Kooser and sponsored by The Poetry Foundation.

"Eagle" first appeared in the anthology *The Night's Magician: Poetry about the Moon* (Negative Capability Press, 2018).

"Bald Eagle" first appeared in *Bright Illuminations: The Art of Margee Bright Ragland and the Words of Others* (The Village Smith Press, 2015).

Section III of "Eagle & Phenix Dam" first appeared as a public art installation by sculptor Mike McFalls, permanently mounted on the mill's retaining wall above the Chattahoochee Riverwalk in Columbus, Georgia.

Thank you, also, to the Jentel Artist Residency Program for allowing me time in Wyoming to work on this book.

And thanks to the following for your continued support of my work: Erika Adams, Anupama Amaran, Jean Arambula, David Bottoms, Justin Briley, Virginia Causey, Jean-Patrick Connerade, Carolyn Folse, Cathy and Fred

Fussell, Mark Halliday, Jeffrey Harrison, Chuck Hemard, Richard Howard, Susan Hrach, Stefka Hrusanova, Judi Livingston, Matthew McCabe, Mike McFalls, Graham Norwood, Natalee Norwood, James Ogburn, Marc and Marleen De Bode Olivié, Melissa Pritchard, Margee Bright Ragland, J. Allyn Rosser, Megan Sexton, Tamma Smith, Scott Wilkerson.

And for support of all kinds, thanks to my families—both born-to and chosen.

About The Author

Nick Norwood's previous collections are *The Soft Blare*, *A Palace for the Heart*, and *Gravel and Hawk*—winner of the Hollis Summers Prize in Poetry—as well as the limited edition books *Text* and *Wrestle* produced in collaboration with the artist and master printer Erika Adams. His poems have appeared widely in such places as *The Paris Review*, *Southwest Review*, *Western Humanities Review*, *Southwestern American Literature*, *Shenandoah*, *Poetry Daily*, *New Ohio Review*, *Five Points*, *The Oxford American*, *The Greensboro Review*, U.S. Poet Laureate Ted Kooser's syndicated column *American Life in Poetry*, on the PBS NewsHour site Art Beat, on NPR's *Writer's Almanac*, and elsewhere. His honors include a Pushcart Prize, an International Merit Award in Poetry from *Atlanta Review*, a residency at the Jentel Foundation in Wyoming, both a Tennessee Williams Scholarship and a Walter E. Dakin Fellowship from the Sewanee Writers' Conference. He has also published a number of essays, reviews, book chapters, and critical studies of poetry. He teaches creative writing at Columbus State University and directs the Carson McCullers Center for Writers and Musicians in Columbus, Georgia, and Nyack, New York.